First published 1998 © Pop Culture

This edition updated and revised © 1999 Bobcat Books/Pop Culture

Created by Pop Culture, published by OZone Books, a division of Bobcat Books,

distributed by Book Sales Ltd, Newmarket Road, Bury St Edmunds, Suffolk IP33 3YB.

Printed in Singapore

The author and publisher have made every effort to contact all copyright holders. Any,

who for whatever reason have not been contacted are invited to write to the publishers

so that a full acknowledgement may be made in subsequent editions of this work.

ISBN 0-7119-7741-0

OZ100155

Picture credits: All Action, Retna Pictures Limited, Starfile

Cover Picture: All Action

Design by: POP CULTURE

21ST CENTURY CELTS

BY MARK FREETH

THE CELTIC CONNECTION

folk music – a forum to express indignation, frustration, anger: 'protest' music. Equally, a means of conveying joy – a celebration of love, life or a culture. When it comes down to it, blues, country & western, rock'n'roll, pop, heavy metal, punk rock hip-hop and dance are all forms of twentieth-century folk music.

Acts with their roots in the folk music of their country have frequently graced the charts – the *Riverdance* phenomenon being a notable recent example. The Waterboys, Clannad, The Pogues and Sinéad O'Connor have all borrowed from their Celtic background and watched record sales soar. As for America: Bob Dylan, Bruce Springsteen and R.E.M. are all testament to the impact which folk music has had on pop and rock. And yet, the words 'traditional folk music' still conjure up tired images of 'worthiness' for today's chart-addicted music fan, to whom ideas of 'roots' and 'tradition' are as irrelevant as yesterday's papers.

So what do we make of a band of musicians which takes traditional 'folk' music, marries it to a bright, 1990's pop sensibility, and walks confidently straight into the charts, without shedding an ounce of credibility?

Ladies and gentlemen, funkateers and folkies alike, I give you The Corrs...

THE RIGHT TIME

THE STORY

A group comprising a brother and three sisters is formed in an idyllic provincial community in rural Ireland. Drawing on their parents' musical background, the photogenic foursome audition for parts in a music-based movie set in Ireland, which goes on to become an international blockbuster. Said band then go on to become a global, multi-million pound success story.

THE LOW DOWN...

Jim Corr is the eldest of the four, born July 31 1964, and is responsible for guitar, keyboards and backing vocals. Sharon, born March 24 1970, adds a deftly played violin and backing vocals; she first started taking violin lessons from a local priest at the age of seven, and she has missed only one lesson in her whole life! The dedication has obviously paid off – as she is now qualified to teach the instrument herself. Caroline, born March 17 1973, provides the rhythm on drums and bodhran, a traditional Irish percussion instrument; multi-talented, she also plays piano. Finally there's the youngest sister, Andrea, born May 17, 1974. Andrea is the source of those exceptional lead vocals, and occasional displays of amazing dexterity on the tin whistle. Two other non-family musicians, Keith Duffy and Connor O'Farrell, join the band live for bass and lead guitar duties respectively.

THE RIGHT TIME

The Corr family grew up in Dundalk in County Louth, a large town situated mid-way between Belfast and Dublin on Ireland's east coast. Ma and Pa Corr supplemented their day jobs by knocking out lively sets of traditional Irish classics and current chart hits in a well-known local band called Sound Affair — Jean on vocals, Gerry playing keyboards. The young Corrs looked on, soaking it all up, subconsciously preparing themselves to assume the performers' mantle and take the genuine love of music inspired by their parents onto an international stage.

As The Corrs themselves later admitted, there really wasn't anything else they would rather be doing than playing music from day one, and they willingly spent all their spare time practising together. With this kind of background — parents already 'in the business', deciding on their chosen career from an early age — they quickly became proficient in their respective instruments. They put the wheels in motion in 1990:

while still at school, they formed a band to try and attract the attention of a crew who were casting for a movie to be set in Dublin. By their own admission, this prototype Corrs (who at one point considered naming themselves Cosmic Egg!) was a rather lukewarm pop outfit — understandable when all four had grown up on a diet of Duran Duran and Phil Collins. It is revealing that, in a recent article in *Tone* Magazine, Jim chose (in no particular order) the following as his all-time top five tunes:

1. 'Can You Dig It' by the Mock Turtles
2. 'Brimful of Asha' (remix) by Cornershop
3. 'Anything' by Jars of Clay
4. 'Video Killed The Radio Star' by Buggles
5. 'Message in a Bottle' by the Police

Hmmm...

THE RIGHT TIME

The film that The Corrs turned up to audition for, along with many other wide-eyed hopefuls, was Alan Parker's adaptation of Roddy Doyle's modern comic masterpiece, *The Commitments*, which went on to become one of the most successful British films ever made. Ironically for The Corrs, the movie tracks the trials and tribulations of a disparate set of characters putting together a soul band in late '80s/early '90s Dublin. "I was always very interested in getting the band together," Jim told Elissa Lawrence of the *Brisbane News* in February 1998. "*The Commitments* was the pivotal thing that got us off our butts to do something about it."

The audition in front of Parker was in itself a significant event, as it was their début live performance. Andrea, with her striking good looks and natural acting ability, landed the film role of the sister to the central character, Jimmy Rabitte, while her brother and sisters secured walk-on parts. Later, Andrea was to land a part in another Parker-directed vehicle, *Evita*, in which she played the 15-year-old mistress of Juan Domingo Peron (Jonathan Pryce) alongside Madonna's Eva. She has also appeared with the other members of The Corrs in an episode of *Beverly Hills 90210*. (Andrea's involvement with the film world looks set to continue: she is to provide the sweet singing voice for the character Kayley, in Warner Brothers' first fully animated movie, *Quest For Camelot*.)

THE RIGHT TIME

During the filming of *The Commitments*, the band met
musician and entrepreneur John Hughes, whose CV included a stint
with earlier popsters, Minor Detail. Hughes was an acquaintance of head
Riverdance honcho, Bill Whelan, who in turn was working for Parker on the film;
thus, Hughes happened to be on the fringes of the set as the fledgling Corrs went
through their paces. The Corrs weren't Hughes's idea of a typical 'rock' band; only Jim had
experience as a gigging musician, having played in a string of no-hope local groups, and the
girls were still at school at the time. But Hughes was so impressed with the charisma of the
foursome that he offered, there and then, to become their manager should they ever decide to go
professional with their music. It wasn't the hardest decision for the band to make, and in due
course, Hughes was in.

And so, the long hard slog began for The Corrs – the demanding task of trawling through any pub
and club that would take them. Hughes had the foresight to film these early days on camcorder,
and it was this footage which eventually made up the majority of a one hour documentary on
The Corrs for RTE called *The Right Time*, which was screened on St. Patrick's Day 1998,
coinciding with the BBC's broadcast of their concert at the Royal Albert Hall.
The Corrs gradually began to refine the raw material they had displayed
back at their first performance in front of Alan Parker, and started
to develop the look and sound of serious pop/folk/rock
contenders.

THE RIGHT TIME

Of course, The Corrs had a good head start – they had grown up together, which obviously stood them in good stead for life on the road. They had been through the petty pecking orders, rivalries and squabbles that all brothers and sisters experience – the kind of experiences that can crop up within the context of a professional travelling band. But living under the same roof as brother and sisters is not quite the same as living in each other's pockets 24 hours a day – performing together, being interviewed and photographed together, and being in business together.

Of course, there are numerous pop music precedents of family bands. Despite the odd hiccup under the spotlight's glare, The Everly Brothers, The Beach Boys, The Bee Gees, The Jackson Five, The Osmonds, Clannad, The Carpenters, Bros, Five Star, and Hanson have all made careers, successful or otherwise, out of the music industry. They have all chosen to embark on the rocky road to fame and fortune with people they already knew inside out, rather than chancing their arm by hooking up with strangers gleaned from music paper classified ads or rehearsal room notice boards. Indeed, The Corrs feel that their success has brought them closer together as a family rather than driving them apart. The band have even been known to take the mickey out of themselves slightly on this subject by occasionally performing a somewhat tongue in cheek version of Sister Sledge's 'We Are Family'.

"People think we must get tired of being with each other all the time, but we enjoy each other's company," Jim told *The Courier Mail's* Bronwyn Marquardt in February 1998. "We have our moments like any other family, but we try to avoid rows and arguments. Sometimes if you're in each other's faces and working, living and performing with every day for weeks at a time it can get hard, but we handle it surprisingly well."

THE RIGHT TIME

It's true to say that the general perception of family bands is one of sickly, sugary sweetness, *à la* The Partridge Family and The Osmonds. "I think we suffered from the idea of family band, Irish family band... what category does a record shop put us in?" Sharon asked Q's David Quantick in early 1998. "OK, they can go with the traditional music, if you're not recognised by folk and you're not recognised by pop then where are you? But it's not so much of a problem now. We've reached number 7 in the album charts in England which is like saying, We're not folk! Not folk, but kin. People do think we live in a big house together playing around the fire, with cows in the kitchen and stuff."

Clannad and The Carpenters offer interesting contrasts to The Corrs: not only are they also examples of sibling outfits, but they both throw different aspects of our own quartet into the light. Whereas Clannad offer the out-and-out traditional Irish Celt approach, The Carpenters – to whom The Corrs have often being compared in terms of songwriting ability – reflect the unashamedly 'pop' element of the Corrs output. And while The Corrs are now major pop contenders, they are fiercely proud of their musical heritage, and have occasionally seen themselves almost as 'ambassadors' for the culture that gave us the likes of Christy Moore, Planxty and The Bothy Band. Indeed, it is The Corrs' more traditional, Celtic-tinged material, rather than their well-known chart-friendly tunes, which often gains the strongest reaction live. By mixing the universal appeal of traditional Irish music with the insistent melody of a pop tune, The Corrs have created an irresistible package, drawing fans from the folk and pop camps alike.

THE POETRY OF SOUND

Fortunately, it wasn't to be too long before The Corrs' potential was recognised by a record label. In 1994, at the request of Jean Kennedy Smith, US ambassador to Ireland and sister to senator Ted Kennedy, the band flew out to the States to liven up Boston's World Cup '94 shindig. She had already seen them perform at Whelan's in Dublin, and, impressed by their spirited performance, thought them ideally suited to perform for the sizeable Irish contingent native to Boston. Unsigned at the time, The Corrs took this golden opportunity to scout for business Stateside and succeeded in attracting the attention of Atlantic executives, Jason Flom and David Foster (a renowned producer, whose work with Michael Jackson, amongst others, is well-documented). No slouches at recognising a breath-taking talent when they saw one, the duo virtually fell over themselves to sign the band there and then to their own Atlantic subsidiary labels, Lava and 143 respectively. The deal was duly signed, sealed and delivered in next to no time, and The Corrs became fully-fledged Atlantic recording artists.

Given that The Corrs were already a pop force to be reckoned with before that trip to the US, why hadn't they been snapped up by a record company in Ireland? Shrewd planning on the part of the band and their management provides the answer. "The problem with Ireland was that, although there was a lot of interest, there's not enough independence for people there to make decisions," Andrea explained to *Dotmusic's* Mike Pattenden in November 1996. "Plus, the sort of money that was on offer wasn't enough for us to launch us on an international scale, so we held out for a US deal."

22

The first fruit of their Atlantic deal came with 1995's *Forgiven, Not Forgotten*. Produced by David Foster with input from Jim Corr, the album is one of extraordinary beauty right from the outset with the simplicity of a lone violin and piano on the short, haunting traditional Celtic instrumental, 'Erin Shore'. This evocative opener merges effortlessly with the intro of the melancholic single and title track, before the song proper – a gorgeous and infectious composition – begins. 'Heaven Knows' follows – confident drums joined again by that spirit-lifting violin announce a modern pop classic. 'Along With The Girls' echoes the opening track, but this time the bodhran and lively tin whistle accompany the violin and piano. Then the neo-rocker, 'Someday' knocks the listener completely off their feet, courtesy of Jim's choppy guitars and Andrea's sultry vocals. The tempo steadies itself with 'Runaway', another single and gentle ballad which highlights another aspect of The Corrs' skills – their delicate, interweaving harmonies. This leads us neatly and smoothly into the sun-splashed, sub-reggae rhythm of 'The Right Time', before we are brought back again to enjoy the sound of traditional Irish instrumentals on the grand, tear-jerking, 'The Minstrel Boy' and the joyous 'Toss The Feathers'; even though the busy violin and shrill tin whistle are joined by drums and guitars here, the overall feel is that of The Corrs returning once more to their ancestral roots. 'Love To Love You' offers more along those catchy pop lines – another fine choice for a single. Then, a rockier, more American element rears its head with 'Secret Life'. The light-hearted instrumental 'Carraroe Jig' takes us to another time and another world, whilst the dreamy 'Closer' maintains the otherworldly state, a sedate offering led by acoustic guitar.

CHAPTER
TWO

THE
POETRY
OF
SOUND

THE
POETRY OF SOUND

The big guitars take over one last time for the
ripping 'Leave Me Alone', before the album closes, as it
started, echoing with the natural lilting charm of 'Erin Shore', this time
extended so we may savour its sad, languid quality.

Overall, it is this lacing of infectious pop classics with traditional gems from The
Corrs' musical inheritance that makes *Forgiven, Not Forgotten* a consummate and stunning
début. No surprise, then, that with the subtle variety of atmosphere, the peerless vocals and
musical excellence, the album should be a massive international seller, shifting well over two
million copies worldwide, and reaching a respectable No. 7 in the UK charts.

However, this initial welcome success was just an aperitif for the impact of The Corrs' follow-up album,
the slightly tougher, more guitar-orientated, *Talk On Corners* — which gave them their first No. 1 in June
1998. It shares the self-same organic, earthy quality as its precursor, but this time The Corrs
displayed a harder, more street-wise attitude — the Celtic-tinged influences being blended and
embedded more in the songs as a whole rather than as separate selections. This may well have
been influenced by the time the band spent on the road since recording *Forgiven Not Forgotten*.

Talk on Corners certainly starts as it means to go on. The opening track, 'Only When I
Sleep', was selected as a single — a slow pop-rocker with a chorus to die for and
the most infectious guitar hook you'll hear in a long time. But that
idiosyncratic violin emerges alongside the familiar rock set-up,
ensuring The Corrs' Celtic sound a place all of its own in
the history book of pop music.

'When He's Not Around', displays those fabulously honeyed harmonies once more, but also picks up on an Alannis Morrissette vibe; this may have something to do with the fact that one of the guest producers on the album is Alannis's co-writer, Glenn Ballard. Incidentally, the album's other producers are David Foster and Jim Corr, manager Hughes, Oliver Leiber – son of legendary songwriter, Jerry – Rick Nowells of Belinda Carlisle fame and Billy

Steinberg, producer of Madonna and The Bangles. A powerful contingent, to say the least!

The song fades, into a brief, traditional violin and bodhran coda before a simple, but effective a cappella announces the entrance of potential single 'What Can I Do', which develops into a sweet and luscious ballad. Another single comes in the shape of probably their best offering yet, 'I Never Loved You Anyway'. The track has the flavour of a Sheryl Crow composition, and features a contagious, spine-tingling chorus; incidentally, 'Anyway' is the first

of two tracks co-written with songwriting legend, lyricist Carole Bayer Sager, the second being 'Don't Say You Love Me'. The spacious, funky pop of 'So Young' finds the band in celebratory mood, both lyrically and musically, whilst the ballad 'Don't Say You Love Me' introduces a more sombre and reflective mood. That contemplative air continues in 'Love Gives Love Takes'; this perfect soundtrack for that Sunday morning feeling introduces a bitter sweet theme which also pervades the pensive 'Hopelessly Addicted'. The album's pop thread is broken for the only time when an ethereal introduction announces the instrumental 'Paddy McCarthy'.

The track retains a sub-dance beat, but a wonderfully vigorous violin and sparkling tin whistle infuse the song with a Celtic air. 'Intimacy' picks up where 'Hopelessly Addicted' left off, providing another slice of forlorn dreaminess. By sharp contrast, the anthemic 'Queen Of Hollywood' has more of an American honky tonk feel, recalling the atmosphere of 'I Never Loved You Anyway'; the lyric provides the album with its title. Once more, there is a short outro of pure traditional fare, before 'No Good For Me' returns to the album's overall mood of melancholic-pop. A real gem closes the work: The Chieftains, old masters of the Celtic folk game, join The Corrs in a re-working of the Jimi Hendrix classic 'Little Wing' – the song gets the full folk treatment, while Jim replicates some of the late, great guitarist's trademark licks. The result is a gentle, psychedelic-folk wonder.

All in all, *Talk On Corners* proves that – though familiar with their folk music antecedents, The Corrs still have a handle on what's going down in the rock and pop world of the Nineties.

The Corrs' singles have also done brisk business wherever they've been released. Until recently, the only exception to this worldwide success was the UK, and a major factor here is that when The Corrs embarked on their chosen profession, the mass media were preoccupied with so-called 'Britpop'. It has always been the case that, when a new music paper-generated fad grabs the headlines and simultaneously snatches the lion's share of record sales, credible music finds it extremely difficult to get even a small look in. Thankfully, these phases are brief and short-lived, and if the serious, longer term outfits grit their teeth and ride it out, their moment of fame will eventually come.

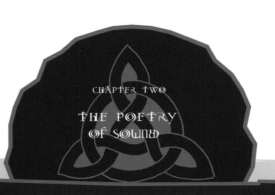
The Corrs' time did come, when in the summer of 1998, the band released their dance-influenced cover of the 1977 Fleetwood Mac classic, 'Dreams', not previously featured on either *Forgiven, Not Forgotten* or *Talk On Corners*. 'Dreams' now features on the more recent copies of the album. The UK finally gave in to the inevitable, and the track reached the No 6 slot in the singles charts. How did they do it? "I suppose it's just spread by word of mouth really," Jim mused to Radio 1's Clive Warren in May 1998. "We did sell an awful lot of our first album here without having had a hit single, but thankfully, we've got a hit single now with 'Dreams'." The song was taken from a tribute album called *Legacy – A Tribute To Fleetwood Mac's 'Rumours'*. The project was put together by Jason Flom and features other luminaries such as Elton John performing 'Don't Stop', Jewel adapting 'You Make Loving Fun' and The Cranberries reworking of 'Go Your Own Way'. Founding Mac member and Corrs fan Mick Fleetwood endorsed the band and their contribution by guesting with them on a couple of dates on their last American tour and at their special St. Patrick's night concert at the Royal Albert Hall.

With 'Dreams', The Corrs finally managed to persuade the UK to get on the bus, albeit with a lively version of someone else's song, stamped with their unmistakable 'Celtpop' seal. Moreover, the band have even better songs waiting in the wings, songs all their own: tracks from *Talk On Corners* like the aforementioned 'So Young', and 'Queen Of Hollywood' are solid-gold potential hits.

THE POETRY OF SOUND

The dance music quality that The Corrs brought to 'Dreams' is a bold move for the band. For although it contains Andrea's distinctive vocals, Sharon's trademark violin sound, and the lush pop sound that The Corrs have made their own, the track marks a step towards introducing a new section of the music-loving public to their work. The single comes complete with four other mixes, but it's the last three that mark the most interesting departure for The Corrs. The 'TNT Pop Extended' and the 'Tee's Club' mixes are slow, drawn-out, magical affairs, retaining the heart of the radio edit and highlighting Sharon's violin before a gentle techno touch enters the mix, ensuring someone somewhere will soon be sampling the track for some hi-NRG club fare. The final 'In House Mix' though is the most radical, being a completely stripped-down workout, devoid of vocals and instrumentation, leaving only a computer-

generated rhythm beat to set light to a throbbing dancefloor. Indeed, some are bound to ask where The Corrs feature in all this. The only adequate response is that music thrives on variety and change: more power to The Corrs for not only extending the boundaries of their art, but also encouraging attention and interest from a new section of fans. "I'm always open to suggestions and ideas," says Andrea, "But it mightn't work out, and you have to be prepared for that."

ALONG WITH THE GIRLS

he Corrs' collective drop-dead gorgeous good looks has been mentioned in virtually every single magazine and newspaper article that has been written about them. It's easy to say that in an ideal world, this would not matter a jot, and that The Corrs should be assessed on their music talents alone. But it would be naïve to suggest that the talented foursome owe their success purely to their musical ability, and that their striking appearance isn't a considerable advantage in the competitive world of pop. Would The Corrs have made it thus far if they had been made up of three very plain Janes and an overweight brother? Possibly. But it would have taken them a damn sight longer. The music business thrives on promoting fantasy figures for the masses to adore – what is pop music at the end of the day except a means of providing an escapist thrill from the mundane routine of everyday life?

It is a strange but true fact that when vanity gets the better of individuals from the rock and pop world and they succumb to the temptation of trying their luck in another escapist medium – film – the results have tended to be disastrous. David Bowie, Mick Jagger, Madonna and Sting are proof that perfectly competent and photogenic musicians do not necessarily make good actors.

This might seem odd on first reflection: one might reasonably expect that the qualities necessary for believable performances on the stage and screen could be found amongst those used to putting on an act in a musical context. But alas, no – roles have been ruined and reputations left in tatters after members of the pop hierarchy have ended up paying a little too much attention to their own press and suffered the consequences on the silver screen.

ALONG WITH THE GIRLS

Thankfully, it's not a problem that The Corrs have to worry about. Andrea has already shown herself to be at perfectly at ease in the small acting roles that she's already undertaken. It is inevitable that Andrea will find herself increasingly in demand for such roles, being the band's lead singer, and thus bearing the brunt of the scrutiny – not for nothing has she been voted 'Sexiest Woman In Ireland'. And this is fine, as we have come to expect so-so looking outfits fronted by stunning individuals. But, dammit, if *all four* of The Corrs don't share those distinctively sculpted features and slim physiques! Yep, even Jim!

Ah, Jim. It may well be considered fortuitous that The Corrs' line-up includes a male – and not some faceless session musician either, but a vital element in performance, songwriting and production, without which, The Corrs' look and sound would be a very different matter altogether. Moreover, despite the fact that The Corrs' music is a million miles away from the likes of The Spice Girls or All Saints, if it wasn't for Jim, the three sisters may well have found themselves fending off inane 'girl group' comments and questions. "It's great," he admitted to *Teletext's* Colin Irwin on 17 May 1998. "I get ignored sometimes by guys ogling the girls, but that's OK. I like being in the shadows. Sometimes it works in reverse and I get more attention because I'm the only guy."

This is not to say that The Corrs aren't a mite fed up with so much attention being placed solely on their looks when they are out there trying to promote their creativity, though it must be said that those figure-hugging long black dresses and immoderate eye make-up have not hindered their progress. The Corrs, like any other major league pop or rock star band, are now being recognised the world over – including some of the more remote corners of the globe – even in disguise!

ALONG WITH THE GIRLS

This problem, along with heavy touring
(both under their own steam and as a support for the likes
of Michael Bolton and Celine Dion) and recording schedules, can
make it difficult to cement serious personal relationships: "It's hard
sometimes," Caroline told Bronwyn Marquardt for the *Belfast Telegraph* in March
1998. "But when your career is important and you love what you do, but your boyfriend
wants you to stop, I don't think he'd be the right person anyway. My boyfriend's career is
important to him so he understands how I feel."

In fact, the pressures of the job have, on occasion, brought The Corrs close to questioning if the
whole thing was worth all the stress: "We tried to travel the whole world at once and nearly ended up
killing ourselves," Andrea told Lee Harpin from *Mega Star*, about successfully completing sell-out tours
around the globe. "I wouldn't change what we did but I wouldn't do it again." But after well-deserved
breaks and seeing their careers and the music business for what it is – a job like any other (albeit not
exactly nine-to-five!), The Corrs have always managed to recharge their low batteries and rekindle their
enthusiasm, return to work like the true professionals they are. They are philosophical about its
drawbacks and enthusiastic about its highs, and they take a remarkably balanced view of the
attention that their good looks has helped to win. "Sex appeal is not something that you can
deny," admitted Sharon to *In Dublin* in October 1997. " 'Looks don't really come into it'?
That, for the want of a better word, is bullshit. Of course people want to see nice
faces, it's only natural. Sex appeal has been part of our success." But,
whenever they get the chance to go home to Ireland, family and
friends in Dundalk help keep the collective Corrs' feet
firmly on the ground.

'Home' could also feasibly include Australia – a country they have come to care for so much, they have adopted it as their second home. Australia has certainly proved very receptive to the band – indeed, it was one of the first countries, along with Japan, in which *Forgiven Not Forgotten* achieved gold status. These two countries were the first to really go overboard about the band, and The Corrs have subsequently made sure they are well catered for on world tours. Moreover, the warm feelings are clearly reciprocated: "It's definitely a mutual love," Andrea told *Brash* magazine in February 1998. "Selling that many records on the other side of the world was just astounding. We love being in Australia. The Barrier Reef, the Sydney Harbour, they're just lovely. It's our biggest market. It's great we do well in Ireland too, because no one likes to be ignored in one's own country but we always say, if things go wrong in Ireland, we can always move to Australia!"

And Australia, where The Corrs' début album has so far gone eight times platinum, would certainly welcome them with open arms.

The fact that there are three women in The Corrs is enough to draw comment from the media. Certainly, the pop scene is well-stocked with female artists at the present time. The ubiquitous Spice Girls and their newest rivals All Saints have both promoted their own ideas of girl power and seen their music storm the pop charts. The twin sisters of Boyzone's Shane Lynch, Keavy and Adele, who make up half of the new, all-Irish girl group, B*witched, have already cited The Corrs as an influence. Clearly the influence has paid off – they shot straight to number one with their very first release, 'C'est La Vie'! And take a look at the all-female Lillith Fair festival – born in the USA, but shortly to take to an international stage – if you need reminding of the extent of 'girl power' in the music world.

ALONG WITH THE GIRLS

So, just how do The Corrs fit into this frame? Well, Andrea, Sharon and Caroline could never be accused of cynically trading on their looks or their sexuality, and they have certainly never been marketed in such a way as to undermine their art or their credibility. The covers of their records simply show the band as they are: four very good looking individuals. They even help to promote Celtic art a little by displaying their distinctly Celtic-flavoured logo. And you are not likely to find any of them semi-naked in the likes of *Loaded* or *FHM*, or exposing details of their private life in print. Unlike other celebrities who seem only too eager to display their dirty laundry in public, there are no sex, drugs and booze scandals attached to The Corrs – they are the perfect role models for a wholesome way of life. "We are essentially private people like our parents." Andrea told Alan Corr (no relation!) for *RTE Guide* in March 1998. "I really don't think our private lives would be interesting enough to talk about. Madonna does that and so does Paula Yates, with us it would be all too boring, it wouldn't make titillating reading. We're musicians so I think why do people want to know all the personal stuff? You can read controversial interviews about people's sex lives but that's how the interviewee wants it to go."

John Hughes has often been quoted as saying, "sex, politics, religion, they're all private", and his attitude is one to which The Corrs firmly adhere. The band have often been asked about their opinions on the Irish troubles, but though they have their views, they choose to keep them out of their songs. As for religion, the band did admit that they were greatly affected when they received the opportunity to meet the Pope: "Whether you're a churchgoer or not, it's a very special occasion," Jim reminded Neil Melloy of *The Courier Mail* in February 1998, "because you're meeting probably the most influential person on the planet. Spiritually, it was a very special moment for all of us. I remember directly afterwards we found it very hard to express our feelings about the moment."

ALONG WITH THE GIRLS

When it comes down to it, The Corrs are a consummately professional act, and their present day achievements are the result of a number of factors. There is their willingness to gig relentlessly in the early days, often to indifferent audiences, driven by a rock-steady self-belief in themselves and their music. Even so, the band remain refreshingly level-headed about their success, and acknowledge that putting on a face for the public can clearly be a strain at times. "I must tell you that I look at something like the MTV Awards and say, 'everybody I see up there is a clown!'" admitted Andrea to Joe Jackson of *Hot Press* in December 1997. "I am a clown. All of us in the music business are clowns. The gear, the outfits, everybody dressing up as if they are part of a circus, craving attention. That's what I see when I look at Prince, with a lollipop in his hand! Or a band like Kiss. We're all clowns. When I look at people like that there definitely is a cringe factor. That's what I see when I look up at a poster of Prince. Yet I also see the vulnerability and know, from myself, the feelings of self consciousness and doubt that are often hidden behind the clown's make-up. People can look at me and say, 'Andrea looks well', while at the same time, I am thinking, 'oh my God, I look like a caricature'. And then all I want to do is take all the make-up off and get away from it all." But The Corrs appear to have calmly taken all this in their collective stride, unfazed by such trivialities, safe in the knowledge that, those people who got on board for all the wrong reasons won't be hanging round for very long anyway, whilst those whose souls have been spoken to by the strains of an almost otherworldly sound, will be with The Corrs for life.

HOPELESSLY ADDICTED

With the wide range of influences that they draw on, it's no surprise that The Corrs often have to field the query, 'Well, exactly what kind of band are you?' "We're a traditional Irish pop-rock band, whatever that is," Caroline told *The Sunday Mail* in October 1997. "It's a blend of modern rhythms and technology with acoustic instruments – violin, tin whistle, drums – and of course, the voices. The marrying of all these elements makes our sound." But The Corrs themselves, at one time or another, must have wondered how the traditionalists viewed their taking raw Irish music into the pop/rock arena; or indeed, how your average pop fan might react to music usually associated with older generations. The band balk at the suggestion that they should, or even could, go one way or the other: "All the elements are essential." Andrea says, "The traditional has a huge draw and it's so lively. The combination of pop, rock, and traditional was a natural progression for us; you can't take one way and say 'that's it'. Along with that, we focus very much on melody, I think good melody is what music is really about." The Corrs need not worry on either count of course – both traditionalists and pop aficionados have warmly embraced the twin elements that make up the band's distinctive sound.

HOPELESSLY ADDICTED

There is not a single community, country or culture in human history that hasn't made music – whether it be with voices or instruments. Music is universal. "If you're happy, you sing with laughter. You always hear old guys whistling in Ireland, walking down the street," Caroline told *Good Times'* Catriona Jackson in February 1998. It has been said that if one has grown up in Ireland, then one cannot escape the pull of traditional Irish music. There is a strong argument for it finding a way into any Irish musician's work at some point, no matter what area of music they work in. One only has to think of the very different talents of Van Morrison, U2 and Sinéad O'Connor to be reminded of the fact. This should come as no surprise to us – music is obviously in their blood – but a particular form of music, a form that is inextricably linked to a wider, older culture, also runs through their veins.

Some of the saddest music in the world has come from Irish ballads, but the melancholy inherent to much traditional folk music is more than matched by the Irish propensity for good time music – the jig or the reel, for instance.

HOPELESSLY ADDICTED

In both cases, it is a folk music of real human emotion, something which The Corrs readily acknowledge. "I think there's something about Irish music," continues Andrea, "There's this honesty about it. It's uplifting. It's fun. It's not pretentious. It's just what it is. Most of all, I think it gives people a good feeling, and who doesn't like a good feeling?"

Simple words, spoken from the heart. Yet the Corrs' singer couldn't have anticipated in her wildest dreams just how many people would go in search of that good, good feeling. Or just how soon...

CELTIC OVERDRIVE

That The Corrs had benefited from their televised appearance on St Patrick's Day, 1998 was beyond doubt. Within three months of the BBC broadcasting their Royal Albert Hall show, the group's spirited (albeit heavily) re-mixed version of Fleetwood Mac's 'Dreams' finally pushed them into the upper echelons of the UK singles chart, peaking at an admirable No 6. Years of hard work, it seemed, were finally starting to pay off. Keen to monopolise on their burgeoning success, the band scored their biggest coup yet with a top-lining appearance at the Fleadh, an Irish-themed music festival held in the grounds of North London's Finsbury Park in June, 1998. As previous headliners of the event included the likes of Van Morrison and Bob Dylan, the little group from Dundalk were now in serious danger of becoming huge stars in their own right. "We try and take every opportunity that comes to us, no matter how small," Caroline once told *Planet Rock Profiles'* Dave Fanning. "We'll just do it and see what happens". Whilst the philosophy was sound enough, those little "opportunities" now involved thousands of people, keen to catch a glimpse of pop music's 'next big thing'. In truth, The Corrs' appearance at the Fleadh marked a major turning point in the group's fortunes. Once dismissed as nothing more than "a pretty version of The Dubliners", they were now one of the UK's more bankable musical commodities, a fact confirmed when their second LP, *Talk On Corners*, finally hit the top of the charts some thirty weeks after it was originally released. To help sales reach this timely crescendo, Atlantic Records had cannily re-packaged the album under the banner, *'Talk On Corners – Special Edition'*, presenting would be buyers with extra tracks – including a modified version of *Forgiven Not Forgotten*'s winsome 'Runaway' – as well as crystalline re-mixes of future singles 'What Can I Do' and 'So Young'. The group's recent hit, 'Dreams' was also added to the LP's track listing to further sweeten the pill. For Jim Corr, reaching the top of the UK charts was something akin to a personal Nirvana: "We've been Number One in Ireland, Spain, Singapore, Malaysia, Australia and New Zealand," he enthused to *Q* magazine, "but it means so much more to be top in England. We've always been avid followers of the English scene and English acts. Watching *Top Of The Pops* was like a religious experience in our house." It was about to become a surreal one too, as the band's next single, 'What Can I Do', allowed them to make the transition from watching the programme to regularly appearing on it. Always a potential chart-topper, 'What Can I Do'

neatly encapsulated The Corrs' principal melodic strengths for all to hear: a gently stroked, yet subtly commanding guitar riff, crisp, non-intrusive percussion and a mournful, bitter-sweet violin all provided a perfect musical backdrop against which Andrea could unwind her melancholic tale of unrequited love and lost opportunity. Celtic to the bone, 'What Can I Do''s yearning simplicity finally gave The Corrs their first self-penned Top Five single hit. By the end of the 1998, the group's follow-up, 'So Young',

imitated its predecessor's success and bounced into the UK singles charts on the back of a particularly pleasing video, allowing viewers to see a more light-hearted side to the four siblings. Standing atop a skyscraper, the girls seemed to be taking inordinate pleasure launching paper planes into the street below while singing the song's up-lifting chorus: "We are so young now, and when tomorrow comes, we'll just do it all again". Jim, it has to be said, looked more bemused than enthralled by his sisters' experiments with rudimentary aviation. Away from all the hits, The Corrs were also forging ahead on the live front, with a much anticipated headlining tour of Great Britain beginning at Nottingham's Royal Court Theatre on December 3. Booked months before *Talk On Corners'* runaway success transformed them into a something of a phenomenon, many of the venues at which the group were scheduled to appear didn't accurately reflect their new-found commercial status. In short, some theatres were

simply too small to accommodate the level of interest shown by the public in the band, and extra dates were hastily added to the itinerary in an effort to keep up with ticket demand. Henceforth, what started life as a semi-modest trawl across the UK soon became a mammoth exercise in group stamina. The Corrs, however, found themselves largely equal to the task, allowing British audiences an opportunity to witness a band on the cusp of superstardom. Aided by the ever reliable Dublin duo of Conor Brady (lead guitar) and Keith Duffy (bass guitar), Ireland's most successful musical export since U2 provided fine drama on a nightly basis, straddling venues as diverse as Glasgow's semi-intimate Clyde Auditorium (December 10/11) and Birmingham's imposing NEC complex (December 22). Aside from the rapturously received – and by now extremely familiar – triumvirate of 'Dreams', 'What Can I Do' and 'So Young', The Corrs continued to mine their Gaelic roots with showy renditions of 'Erin Shore', 'Toss The Feathers' and the ever-popular 'Haste To The Wedding'. There was even time for a few solo spots, with Jim taking a semi-comedic turn at the piano before being joined on stage by sisters Caroline and Sharon for a sensitive reading of Jimmy McCaffrey's 'No Frontiers'.

Though the tour would roll inexorably on into March of 1999 (including five sold out nights at London's prestigious Wembley Arena), an apt reward for the band's punishing schedule thus far came at the end of December, 1998, when it was announced that *Talk On Corners* had become the UK's best selling album of the year, shifting some 1.8 million copies. "We have worked so, so hard to get to where we've got to," said Jim at the time. "We honestly couldn't have anticipated that we would have the number one selling album of the year, so we're now experiencing the fruits of our labour." The Corrs' domination of the UK music scene was driven home with compelling force in February, 1999, when the quartet beat off stiff competition from Air, The Beastie Boys, The Fun Lovin' Criminals and R.E.M to take home the title of 'Best International Group' at the annual Brit Awards. The band's acceptance speech, however, showed little sign that all the recent success had gone to their heads: "We're absolutely thrilled and delighted," enthused Caroline from the podium, "and want to thank the fans and the people who voted for us. Last but not least, thanks to our parents Jean and Gerry, and also our manager John Hughes." Within minutes of being presented with the award, The Corrs once again took to the stage, this time to perform a flirtatious version of 'Haste To The Wedding' and also plug their new single, the gentile ballad 'Runaway'. Inevitably, 'Runaway' – or to give it its proper title, 'Runaway (Tin Tin Out Remix)' – débuted at No 2 in the charts the following week. The award bestowed upon The Corrs at The Brits bash was actually the second they had received in recent months. In fact, the band had also been honoured at Belgium's IFPI Platinum Europe Awards in July, 1998.

Yet, unlike many of their musical contemporaries, they were neither embarrassed nor irritated by 'corporate gong shows'. "Without wanting to get egotistical about it," reasoned Jim, "I think success has got to be celebrated. It takes an enormous amount of hard work to sell a million records, and the few awards that come your way are always very gratifying to get." If anyone sought further confirmation that The Corrs now ruled the roost of British pop, it came on March 17, 1999, when prominent music channel *VH-1* set aside their usual programming schedule in favour of 'Corrs Day' – a 24 hour celebration of all things Corr, with numerous videos, documentaries and select live footage of the group's appearance at 1998's Fleadh festival all on show. Of particular interest to fans was the 'Ten Of The Best' section, where Sharon, Caroline, Andrea and Jim were allowed to collectively pick ten videos that represented their own musical tastes. Whilst Sharon's choice of U2's 'One' and Jim's championing of The Police's 'Walking On The Moon' were hardly surprising in view of previous statements

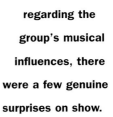

CHAPTER FIVE
CELTIC OVERDRIVE

regarding the group's musical influences, there were a few genuine surprises on show. Caroline, for instance, demonstrated extremely good taste by plumping for Kate Bush's ethereal ballad 'The Man With The Child In His Eyes', whilst Andrea confounded expectation with her choice: To wit, Prince's 'Alphabet Street'. "I chose it because it has a lot of memories," she confessed to viewers. "I remember our daddy confiscated my album (*Lovesexy*), not because Prince was nude on the cover, but because he heard me playing another album of his where the lyrics were even nastier! So Daddy actually confiscated the wrong album. But he only knows that now..." Somewhat inevitably, the positivism surrounding The Corrs' rapid ascent to stardom brought many a cynic out of the woodwork. It seemed that for every compliment the group received in the press, for every record sold, a vigorous counter-argument against them was duly launched. Some of the criticism raised

was hardly new, with sound-bites such as "saccharine-sweet sentimentality" and "moderately talented wood-nymphs" recalling the more unkind reviews that accompanied the band's first album and formative live shows. Nonetheless, the one charge The Corrs continued to face more than any other was that they had risen to international prominence on the back of their looks. It was a viewpoint they were heartily aware of, yet still keen to defend: "If we all had torn jeans and greasy hair," reasoned Caroline, "and didn't look so pretty, the expectations would be different." Simple genetics, it seemed, had provided nay-sayers with a convenient stick with which to beat the group's accomplishments. Of course, it was prudent to suggest that The Corrs' striking demeanour was no hindrance to their commercial appeal, and equally, there was no denying they had used their looks to their advantage. Yet, aside from donning paper bags over their heads or resorting to wearing the odd potato sack, there was now precious little the group could do to reverse certain critics' perceptions of them. One instinctively felt though, that no matter how successful The Corrs became, they would always be at the mercy of those who equated personal attractiveness with a lack of talent. The antidote to any negative criticism often lies in establishing credibility with one's peers, and The Corrs' next move was certainly a step in the right direction. In April 1999, Ireland's most enduring, and indeed, respected traditional folk group, The Chieftains, released their

latest album, *Heart Of Stone*. A sterling effort that celebrated "a woman's view of love through Irish traditional song", the LP was notable for the fact that Chieftains' leader Paddy Moloney had managed to assemble some of rock's most distinguished female talents to help him realise his musical vision. Aside from native Celts such as Sinead O'Connor and Loreena McKennitt, American blues icon Bonnie Raitt and jazz diva Joni Mitchell also made contributions to the project. As did a little known group named The Corrs. In fact, the quartet's rousing treatment of Mary O'Hara's 'I Know My Love' was actually one of *Heart Of Stone*'s more enjoyable moments. By infusing a traditional Irish love song with a distinctly Latin feel, The Corrs managed to breathe new life into old bones. Initially, however, the band were more than a little surprised by Paddy Moloney's suggestion to take the track 'Down Mexico Way': "I sent them a tape of the song, by an old singer... I think it was Mary O'Hara," Moloney confirmed to *Mojo*'s Colin Irwin, "and they didn't believe I was serious. They prepared something else instead. But I'd just been doing an album called *Santiago* and had these Galacian rhythms in my head. So when I explained I wanted to put this beat behind them, they loved it!"

By the Spring of 1999, The Corrs' second album, *Talk On Corners*, was well on its way to selling 2.5 million copies in the UK alone. If one added platinum discs from Australia, New Zealand, Ireland and The Far East, the group's sales tally from some fifteen songs was nothing short of staggering. Nonetheless, there was one territory left to conquer. Predictably, it was also the biggest, potentially the most lucrative, and notoriously choosy about whom it took to its heart. Undeterred, Sharon, Jim, Andrea and Caroline got on the plane in search of America.

Before The Corrs had even set foot on US soil, their manager, John Hughes, had been busy ensuring that their short promotional visit in support of the American release of *Talk On Corners* elicited maximum impact for his charges. Therefore, the group had been lined up to appear on some of The States' most notable, and heavily watched, TV shows. In little under two weeks, The Corrs dutifully plied their wares on *The Rosie O'Donnell Show*, *Saturday Night Live*, *Late Night With David Letterman* and rather impressively, *The Today Show*, which boasts the highest audience rating for a breakfast programme anywhere in the world. By the end of week one, the group had reached an estimated audience of no less than 50 million Americans.

According to Sharon, The Corrs' US campaign was a little late in coming, especially in light of the fact that the group had garnered good reviews when supporting rock legends The Rolling Stones on a string of East Coast dates only a year before. "If only we'd had time then, to come over and tour," she lamented, "but you can only be in so many places at once." Still, the buzz generated by the quartet's flying visit was excellent, and they even managed to fit in a well-attended show at New York's Roseland Ballroom for some 3,000 early US converts to their cause.

Meanwhile, back in the UK, the group's star was continuing to rise. Not content with owning just one of their albums, the British public had gone in frantic search of more Corrs related product. The

result was the re-appearance of the band's first LP, *Forgiven, Not Forgotten*, in the UK Top Ten nearly four years after it originally hit the shops. As this book goes to press, both Corrs records continue to dominate the album charts, consistently orbiting the top five positions. If one adds their recent capture of a lucrative sponsorship deal from Pepsi to the pot, the band's collective earnings in 1999 might well rival that of pop music's biggest money-spinners, The Spice Girls.

Perhaps though, the most indicative aspect of The Corrs' continuing success lies in the fact that both journalists and the general public are beginning to distinguish them as individual personalities as well as a group unit. Sharon seems to have picked up the mantle of "the wise one", no doubt in deference to her serious on-stage demeanour, and the fact that at 28 years of age, she is the eldest of the three sisters. Meanwhile, Jim is being modelled, in some quarters at least, as group leader – a man ever destined to keep an eye on the overall direction of the band, as well as monitor all the unwelcome attention his siblings are subjected to. It must be a hard job.

As far as the younger members of the Corrs family are concerned, the world would appear to be their oyster. Not a day goes by without some reference in the press to how "immensely likeable" Caroline Corr really is. And it has to be said, that behind that energetic drumming style lies a keen sense of humour. Asked recently what she would be doing on the occasion of her 27th birthday (St Patrick's Day, incidentally), the reply given was hardly in keeping with the group's lambent image: "What'll I be doing? Drinking copious amounts of alcohol, I hope!"

Inevitably, the majority of journalistic attention seems to have focused itself squarely on Andrea Corr's shoulders. As lead singer and "face" of the group, her comings and goings have given the tabloids many a headline since the start of 1999. First, it was rumoured that the Corrs' youngest member was dating ex-Spice Girls manager, Simon Fuller. But Fleet Street really went into overdrive when Andrea was captured on film leaving a Dublin restaurant with the 'enfant terrible' of British pop, the ubiquitous Robbie Williams. Unfortunately for the 25-year-old, much of her

growing up will be now done in public. Still, she seems more than up to the task. "I guess there's things I'm missing, but I'm gaining so much more," Andrea recently confessed to *Q*. "I have to say I've never felt so content and so on a level as I do right now."

In just over a year, The Corrs have graduated from moderate pop success to full-on, in your face superstardom. That they have achieved this without resorting to Oasis-like rubbishing of their competition, public spats akin to The Spice Girls and All Saints, or aligning themselves to any particular movement – Britpop, for instance – remains to their enduring credit.

What they choose to offer instead, is a return to the age old notion of melody, where the tune is all important, either in the form of sad-eyed lament, or joyous celebration. In this, they remain quintessentially Irish. "The Corrs' sound is a mixture of music that we like to listen to and music we like to play – traditional, pop and rock," Sharon once confessed. "We've also been classically influenced, so sometimes you'll hear hints of that. But really, it's a mesh of the type of music *we* like to hear."

As the millennium approaches, it seems certain that The Corrs will lead Irish music's charge into the next century. Talented, tuneful, and undeniably attractive, they are as good a collective ambassador as the Emerald Isle might find. "Remarkably rhythmic and wholesomely raunchy," The Corrs have truly earned the nick-name "21st Century Celts"...

UK DISCOGRAPHY

(All on Atlantic/Lava/143 Records,
followed by catalogue number)

ALBUMS

Forgiven Not Forgotten (7567-92612-2)
Talk On Corners (7567-83051-2)

SINGLES

Forgiven, Not Forgotten (A5687CD)
Runaway (A5727CD)
Love to Love You (A561CD)
Only When I Sleep (AT0015CD)
I Never Loved You Anyway (AT0018CD)
Dreams (AT0032CD)
What Can I Do (August '98)

ACKNOWLEDGEMENTS

Thanks to: Juanita, Scott, Paul Flower, Ed and Jo @ EastWest, Zi and Acrelda @ Power, and websites www.atlantic-records.com, www.ubl.com, www.julienas.ipt.univ-paris8.fr, www.pronet.net.au, www.geocities.com/Vienna/Strasse/5608, www.members.xoom.com, www.indigo.ie, www.thecorrs.org, www.wilma.com Grateful thanks to *Q, Mojo, Planet Rock Profiles*, Johnny Vaughan and Heat.

In addition, the following publications have proved useful in the origination of this book:

Brisbane News, Brash ,The Courier Mail, The Sunday Mail, Good Times, Mega Star Belfast Telegraph, Teletext, BBC Radio 1, Q, Dotmusic, In Dublin, RTE Guide, Hot Press, Tone Magazine.